The AMERICAN DISCOVERY ★ TRAIL ★

Explorer's Guide

The AMERICAN DISCOVERY TRAIL

Explorer's Guide

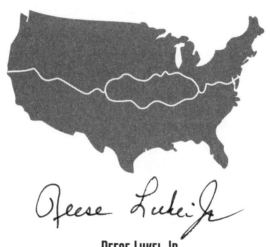

REESE LUKEI, JR.
GENERAL EDITOR

A CORDILLERA GUIDE
JOHNSON BOOKS: BOULDER

9 8 7 6 5 4 3 2 1

Cover design by Margaret Donharl

Library of Congress Cataloging-in-Publication Data

The American Discovery Trail explorer's guide / Reese Lukei, general
    editor. — 1st ed.
       p. cm.
    "A Cordillera Press guidebook."
    Includes index.
    ISBN 1-55566-135-1
    1. American Discovery Trail—Guidebooks.   I. Lukei, Reese.
E160.A54 1995
917.304'928—dc20   95-3143
                                           CIP

American Discovery Trail® and the ADT logo are registered trademarks
of the American Hiking Society.

Printed in the United States by
Johnson Printing
1880 S. 57th Court
Boulder, CO 80301

Contents

Foreword
by Senator Hank Brown, Colorado

It was an honor to sponsor legislation to authorize the study of the American Discovery Trail, our nation's first coast-to-coast hiking trail. While the Appalachian, Continental Divide, and Pacific Crest trails each provide hiking opportunities for traversing the United States from north to south, we lack an east to west "backbone" to link these trails. The American Discovery Trail, totaling over 6,000 miles in length, will serve as this backbone.

The ADT will give the American people greater access to some of our country's most beautiful scenic vistas and historically significant sites. From coast to coast, people will be able to hike, bike, horseback, or simply stroll through the history of our country along canal towpaths, abandoned railroad grades, and such historic pioneer routes as the Pony Express, California, and Santa Fe trails.

One lesser known benefit of our national trails system is the economic impact trails have on neighboring communities. Trails encourage individual fitness, but they also positively impact property values, contribute to small business revenues, and promote tourism.

It is my hope that the American Discovery Trail will foster increased appreciation of and responsibility for our public lands, as well as a heightened awareness of our natural and cultural heritage.

HikaNation arriving at the U.S. Capitol. This group, sponsored by the American Hiking Society, hiked from the Pacific near San Francisco to Cape Henlopen, Delaware, in 1980–81. Parts of their route are used by the ADT. Reese Lukei, Jr.

U.S. Capitol, Washington, D.C. Reese Lukei, Jr.

Foreword
by Former Congresswoman
Beverly Byron, Maryland

At 3:30 on the morning of October 5, 1992, I rose to address the United States House of Representatives for the final time. I was attempting to obtain passage of a bill introduced by Senator Hank Brown and me, H.R. 3011, to authorize a National Park Service feasibility study of the American Discovery Trail. It was the last hours of the last day of the last session of my last term as a member of Congress. It was both an emotional moment and a fitting conclusion. I had been involved in politics for four decades; however, my family commitment to hiking and physical fitness went back even further.

As with any great undertaking, a host of people brought me to that moment: the ADT exploration team, the American Hiking Society and trail coordinator Reese Lukei, *Backpacker* magazine, Senator Brown, and even President Bush. But there I stood, alone with this responsibility. We cut and pasted and passed the bill at 6:30 AM.

It is my fondest hope that my final legislative effort will help pave the way for thousands of Americans to rediscover their country. From day-trippers to coast-to-coast hikers, the ADT holds the promise of showcasing the cultural diversity and scenic beauty of our nation. It is your turn now. I hope that you will be active in the effort to help the American Discovery Trail become America's newest national trail. Take advantage of the hiking opportunities offered by the ADT, but also take part in its care. Have a great hike!

Point Reyes
National
Seashore

San
Francisco

Denver

Omaha

Kansas City

St. Louis

Cincinnati

Cape Henlopen
State Park

Washington, D.C.

About This Guide

"The purpose of this Act is to provide the means for attaining . . . a national system of recreation, scenic and historic trails."

—The National Trails System Act

The American Discovery Trail Explorer's Guide is intended to give the reader an overview of where the trail is located, to identify some of the natural, cultural, historic, and scenic features along and near its route, and to identify some of the people and organizations that have had a role in bringing the ADT from a dream to a trail that millions of Americans can use and enjoy.

This is not a step-by-step guide—a detailed five-volume guidebook series is under development and will be published as the trail is completely located and marked—but this guide, along with maps being produced by Trails Illustrated, can be used to begin your explorations of the ADT. About 2,000 miles of the route is currently marked with ADT trail signs, and more miles are being signed as permission is received to put up trail markers. The route has been designed to provide a continuous footpath for hikers from coast to coast. Many parts can also be used by bicyclists and horse riders where such use is allowed. Some sections are accessible to Americans with disabilities.

This guide has been written from east to west, which is essentially how our nation was settled by the various ethnic and cultural groups that made their way westward. The ADT begins in Delaware near the location of our nation's first Dutch settlement, passes the birthplace or homesite of several of our presidents, wanders through some of our most productive farmland, winds through some of our largest cities (mostly on trails), traverses some of our most magnificent landscapes, crosses part of our most arid desert land, and visits many small communities.

What the ADT does best is to provide the link between the trails in our cities and smaller towns to the more remotely located trails in our forests and mountains. The ADT ties the Appalachian Trail in the east to the Pacific Crest Trail in the west and to the North Country and Continental Divide trails located in the central states.

These long-distance trails are linked with regional trails such as the Bay Area Ridge Trail, Colorado Trail, Katy Trail, Gateway Trailnet, North Bend Rail-Trail, and C & O Canal Trail. Local trails tie into the "system" by providing walks through parks, along waterfronts, and past many of our frequently visited historic sites. The ADT provides the opportunity to travel parts of the routes used by the pioneers and tradesmen who settled our country and links these immigrant and commerce trails into a nationwide system—a system of "Trails for All Americans."

HikaNation arriving in D.C. Reese Lukei, Jr.

Developing the ADT

*"The creation of a true national system of trails begins with
all Americans in their own backyards."*
—Trails for All Americans report

The American Hiking Society and *Backpacker* magazine began
planning the American Discovery Trail in fall 1989. Proponents
envisioned a new, long-distance trail which would be a continuous
multi-use hiking path extending across the United States from one
coast to the other. It would link cities and wilderness, deserts and
forests, people and communities. From the beginning, the idea was
to make the trail accessible to people, so it passes through metropolitan areas and incorporates many urban and rural trails—not
only for hiking, but also for bicycles and horses where local trails
have been designed for such use.

The National Trails System Act, signed into law by President Johnson in 1968, calls for a national system of trails. The Appalachian and
Pacific Crest trails were the first components of this system. The act
encourages the development of additional trails, especially trails
near urban areas of the nation, but also within scenic areas and along
historic travel routes. To date there are eight National Scenic Trails,
eleven National Historic Trails, and over seven hundred National
Recreation Trails in the National Trails System.

The element that has been missing in order to create a system of
these many trails is that they, for the most part, are not connected.
There is some overlap and crossing, particularly of National Historic Trails, but the National Scenic Trails have developed mainly as
north-south trails that follow mountain ranges or other land formations. A principal goal of the ADT has been to connect as many of
these national trails and local and regional trails as possible in order
to complete a system of trails. The ADT connects six National Scenic
Trails, ten National Historic Trails, and twenty-three National Recreation Trails. Hopefully, other new long-distance trails will continue this effort in the future.

During the past twenty-five years there have been many new
developments that have had an effect on trails and the people who
use them. With a greater awareness of the benefits of outdoor
exercise to our personal health and a greater awareness of our

environmental surroundings, people have discovered trails in ever growing numbers. Recognizing this, the Presidents' Commission on Americans Outdoors in 1988 called for the creation of a vast network of hiking and jogging trails, bikeways, and bridle paths. The commission envisioned a nationwide system of trails that would "tie this country together with threads of green," linking communities and providing access to the natural world. The goal is the creation of a network of trails so extensive that all Americans can reach a trail within fifteen minutes of their home or work place. One of the major objectives of the American Hiking Society is to help achieve this goal of "Trails for All Americans."

A large part of the effort to bring trails closer to where people live and work has been the conversion of abandoned railroad rights-of-way into multi-use trails. Currently, there are more than 650 of these trails with 7,200 miles of pathways, offering gentle grades and easy access to millions of Americans. There are another six to seven hundred rail-trails in various stages of development. The ADT has become a part of over thirty of these trails. Another type of trail development that has brought trails closer to people are trails in our cities, especially along riverfronts. The ADT has become a part of many of these trails.

The American Discovery Trail is an outgrowth of this intense interest in trails. As this book goes to press the National Park Service is conducting a feasibility study to determine if the ADT qualifies to become a nationally recognized trail under the National Trails System Act. The National Scenic Trails were envisioned and have developed primarily as trails that provide a remote wilderness experience for the user.

The ADT is also located in such places, but it also provides the opportunity to experience urban and metropolitan trails. The American Hiking Society is proposing that a new category of national trail be created under the National Trails System Act that will give equal recognition to the significance of the urban and metropolitan trails that have developed in the past twenty-five years, and offer encouragement for the development of other extended trails such as the ADT. This new category would recognize that the experience of using and enjoying trails that are close to home is equally as important as remote wilderness trails. It would provide the opportunity to link wilderness and historic trails to the urban and metropolitan trails forming a truly nationwide system of connected trails.

Delaware

The American Discovery Trail (ADT) has its eastern terminus at Cape Henlopen State Park in Delaware on the Atlantic Ocean at the mouth of Delaware Bay. It is appropriate that the ADT begins in the state which on December 7, 1787, became the first to ratify the U.S. Constitution. The route of the ADT through Delaware travels about 45 miles of sidewalks and rural roads, most with paved shoulders. The trail passes through the towns of Lewes, Milton, and Bridgeville, but is mostly in open farmland.

The Cape Henlopen Trailhead overlooks the Atlantic Ocean in Cape Henlopen State Park. Jim Ippolito.

One last look back at Cape Henlopen State Park as you head west. Jim Ippolito.

The scouting team passes by the Zwaanendael Museum in Lewes on their way to Cape Henlopen State Park. Reese Lukei, Jr.

Cape Henlopen is located near Lewes, the 1631 site of the first Dutch settlement in America called Zwaanendael, "Valley of the Swans." Settlers from Holland intended to establish an agricultural and whaling industry, but when Captain David Pietersen de Vries arrived a year later, he found the town deserted. Today, the settlement is commemorated by the DeVries Monument and the Zwaanendael Museum in Lewes.

Cape Henlopen State Park is a very popular area for swimming, fishing, and camping. In 1993, there were over 480,000 visitors. The Seaside Nature Center is open year-round and maintains a register for those traveling on the ADT. The American Discovery Trail begins on the beach near the bunker overlook. During World War II, the park was the site of an U.S. Army coastal fort. Several of the fortifications are still in place, including the bunker, which is an

The town of Milton is one of the picturesque, historic towns the ADT passes through in Delaware. Jim Ippolito.

West of Bridgeville, the ADT travels rural roads which pass through agricultural fields and mixed woodlands. Jim Ippolito.

excellent location from which to watch ship traffic entering and leaving Delaware Bay. There is a sign at the bunker marking the location as the eastern terminus of the ADT.

Upon leaving Cape Henlopen State Park you pass the Cape May/Lewes Ferry, which crosses Delaware Bay to Cape May, New Jersey. The ADT stays on the main road through Lewes, a growing town of about 2,500 people. Ice-cream fans will find their way to Kings Homemade Ice Cream, and the town has several motels.

After a short section along busy U.S. 9, which has a wide paved shoulder, the route follows country roads into Milton. This town, located on the Broadkill River, was the shipbuilding capital of Delaware in the 1800s. It is the site of many fine Victorian mansions and another Kings Homemade Ice Cream. Prime Hook National Wildlife Refuge is a few miles east of Milton and makes an interesting side trip for those who enjoy birdwatching.

After leaving Milton the ADT follows rural roads through farmland. Soon after crossing U.S. 113, the trail passes through Redden State Forest, which offers primitive camping. Continuing west on rural roads the route crosses U.S. 13, the principal north-south highway on the eastern shore of Delaware, Maryland, and Virginia. The trail enters Bridgeville, a town of 1,500 people and the agriculture and railroad center for the region. Bridgeville has a bed and breakfast.

The ADT follows country roads through the unincorporated towns of Cocked Hat, Adamsville, and Hickman and leaves Delaware on Rural Road 113, which becomes Hobbs Road in Maryland. The boundary between Delaware and Maryland is part of the Mason-Dixon Line.

The harbor at Annapolis, Maryland. Annapolis and Anne Arundel County Conference and Visitors Bureau.

Maryland

The Maryland ADT begins on Hobbs Road in an area known as Ringgolds Green, a former community rich with folklore and ghost stories. After passing through the unincorporated community of Hobbs, the trail soon enters Denton, the county seat of Caroline County. Martinak State Park and Camp Mardela, privately operated, have camping. The ADT route through Denton and Caroline County has been well marked by members of Boy Scout Troop 165.

From Denton the route continues on rural, lightly traveled roads through Ridgely to Tuckahoe State Park. This 1,800-acre park has campsites and a lake for fishing. Queenstown has a country market and two bed and breakfast inns. South of Queenstown is the Wye Island Natural Resource Management Area, a 2,500-acre protected area offering hiking, birding, and water-oriented activities. At Grasonville and Stevensville you have entered Chesapeake Bay country where you have the choice of many fine seafood restaurants. There are also motels and many fast food options.

At Stevensville arrangements must be made for a taxi or a friendly motorist to carry you across the Chesapeake Bay Bridge. Pedestrians and bicycles are not permitted on the bridge except one day each year, usually in April. At the western end of the bridge, Sandy Point State Park offers camping.

Annapolis, located on the Severn River, is the capital of Maryland and the site of the U.S. Naval Academy. It is a small historic city that has been able to retain its southern character. When it was designated a National Historic Landmark, Interior Secretary Stewart Udall noted that "Annapolis has the greatest concentration of eighteenth-century buildings anywhere in the United States." Annapolis has always been a maritime center. Today, it attracts pleasure boaters from nearby metropolitan centers and is a major port on the inland waterway that extends along the Atlantic coastline from New England to the Gulf of Mexico.

The current route from Annapolis to Bowie is on two-lane roads south of U.S. 50. The Washington, Baltimore, and Annapolis railtrail is planned for completion in 1997 and this trail, known as the

South Shore Trail, will become the permanent ADT route into Odenton and then into Bowie. Bowie is known as the cradle of American horse racing and is the home of three triple crown winners from the Woodward Stables.

Between Bowie and Greenbelt the route goes through the Beltsville Agricultural Center, a 7,000-acre working farm with experimental agricultural projects. There are two visitor centers in this area: the U.S. Department of Agriculture National Visitor Center, where you can see examples of various products that were tested here and that are in daily use today, and the U.S. Department of Interior National Wildlife Visitor Center, which has many interactive scientific and environmental exhibits.

Greenbelt is one of the first "planned" cities built in the 1930s during the New Deal. The city got its name from the greenbelt of

C & O Canal near Great Falls, Maryland. Reese Lukei, Jr.

Great Falls Tavern & Locks on the C & O Canal, Maryland. Reese Lukei, Jr.

undeveloped land surrounding the community. A short distance from here is Goddard Space Flight Center, which has a visitors center and offers prearranged tours of the facility. Goddard is unique among NASA centers in being able to handle, inhouse, the complete cycle of building a spacecraft from conception through fabrication and testing. Greenbelt Park, a National Park Service unit, has camping and several hiking trails.

From Greenbelt Park follow the Anacostia stream valley to the Washington, D.C., boundary. The route from Greenbelt is on a paved off-road trail along the levee to Bladensburg. About midway, at College Park, there are views of the oldest continuously operated airport in the United States, which also has an aviation museum. The Wright brothers and Amelia Earhart flew out of here. Lake Artemesia has a 2-mile perimeter walk around the lake and picnic facilities. Just before entering Bladensburg, the route becomes the Northwest Branch Trail into Chillum Park, where you enter Washington, D.C., at Sixteenth Street. From here, follow the historic Fort Circle Trail on sidewalks to Rock Creek Park.

During the Civil War, sixty-eight forts encircled the District of Columbia to protect it from Confederate armies. This ring of forts was along Military Road which the ADT follows. At Thirteenth Street are the partially reconstructed ramparts of Fort Stevens, and at Third Street is a park that was the site of Fort Slocum. Just off Military Road you enter Rock Creek Park and follow the blue-blazed trail on the east side of Rock Creek. Plan to stop at the Glover-Archibald Nature and Visitor Center as you enter the park.

The route through Washington, D.C., provides several opportunities to take side trips to visit the Mall area with the Capitol, White House, Washington Monument, Smithsonian Institution, and other points of interest. The ADT follows the towpath along the Chesapeake and Ohio Canal from the Georgetown section of Washington, D.C., to Oldtown, Maryland, for 167 miles. The C & O Canal is a national historic park that parallels the Maryland shore of the Potomac River for 184 miles from Washington, D.C., to Cumberland, Maryland. The canal was in operation from 1850 to 1924 when it was closed after sustaining severe damage from major flooding. Campsites for hikers and bicyclists are located about every 5 miles beginning at milepost 25 and westward. The Potomac Heritage National Scenic Trail also follows the C & O Canal towpath.

There are many attractions along the towpath. At Great Falls and Georgetown, canal boat rides are available during spring and summer. A recently reconstructed boardwalk allows a visit to the very edge of the spectacular Falls of the Potomac at Great Falls. Harpers Ferry National Historic Park on the West Virginia side of the canal is where the Appalachian Trail crosses the ADT. The Appalachian Trail Conference headquarters is located in Harpers Ferry. Virginia, West Virginia, and Maryland come together here at the confluence of the Potomac and Shenandoah rivers.

Antietam National Battlefield near milepost 69 was the site of the bloodiest one-day battle of the Civil War. The 3,118-foot-long Paw Paw Tunnel at milepost 156 was the most ambitious and expensive achievement of the canal company. The ADT crosses the Potomac River into West Virginia on a privately owned wooden bridge; the toll is twenty cents.

The Chesapeake and Ohio Canal was once an important waterway running 184 miles from Georgetown to Cumberland, Maryland. Seventy-four locks lifted boats a total of 609 feet. Today, hikers and cyclists enjoy the towpath. Reese Lukei, Jr.

Dolly Sods, in the Monongahela National Forest, West Virginia, at sunrise. Reese Lukei, Jr.

Looking out from one of the tunnels on the North Bend Rail-Trail. North Bend Rail-Trail Foundation.

West Virginia

In West Virginia, the American Discovery Trail ventures through what might be termed the "amazement park" of eastern America. Many trails offer scenic vistas, pastoral settings, stirring waterfalls, and botanical diversification, while rivers provide for whitewater rafting, kayaking, canoeing, and sternwheel pleasures. There are also caves for underground exploring; cliffs for climbing; and friendly people to assure success in your trekking adventures. West Virginia has the natural assets for a multi-faceted outdoor visit.

After crossing the Potomac River, the ADT follows a lightly used road to Green Spring. This segment of the ADT follows a valley of the Appalachian Mountain Range, then crosses a mountain near the Springfield Public Hunting and Fishing Area to Fort Ashby. Still on a valley road, the ADT passes the Nancy Hanks Memorial, the birthplace of Abraham Lincoln's mother. At Greenland Gap, the Nature Conservancy operates a nature preserve. This is a part of

One of ten tunnels on the North Bend Rail-Trail. North Bend Rail-Trail Foundation.

Bikers on a trail through the woods, West Virginia. North Bend Rail-Trail Foundation.

the Potomac Highlands, some of the oldest mountains and hardwood forests in the world.

Continuing south on country roads the ADT passes through the town of Scherr and on to Jordan Run and U.S. Forest Service Road FR75, which climbs steeply onto the Allegheny Front in Monongahela National Forest. At 3,500 to 4,000 feet, this segment is the highest elevation that the ADT will reach east of the Rockies. The ADT traveler will soon know why West Virginia is called the Mountain State!

The Dolly Sods National Wilderness Area is unique in that it resembles the Canadian tundra. It can snow here during any month of the year. This raised plateau provides panoramic vistas of the Allegheny Mountains. On a dirt road the ADT goes south from Bear Rocks past Red Creek Campground, then descends to Laneville and through Canaan Valley Resort State Park. The ADT intersects the 290-mile Allegheny Trail at Canaan Valley and follows it to Blackwater Falls State Park. The park gets its name from the five-story-high falls on the Blackwater River as it tumbles down Blackwater Canyon. Still in the Monongahela National Forest the ADT continues on to Hendricks. From Hendricks to Parsons the route will be on the Dry Fork Rail-Trail. Country roads provide the route to Nestorville, through Moatsville to Tygart Lake State Park.

Harpers Ferry, West Virginia, where the Shenandoah River meets the Potomac. Reese Lukei, Jr.

Blackwater Falls on the Blackwater River, West Virginia. Reese Lukei, Jr.

Grafton is the location of the International Mother's Day Shrine, which was the site of the first observance of Mother's Day on May 10, 1908. The route to Valley Falls State Park is on country roads, then from Spelter to Clarksburg the ADT follows the Harrison County Rail-Trail. Clarksburg is the birthplace of General Thomas J. "Stonewall" Jackson. Over 40 percent of the population is of Italian descent and each Labor Day the West Virginia Italian Heritage Festival is held here.

From Wolf Summit for the next 60 miles to Walker, the ADT follows the North Bend Rail-Trail, a National Recreation Trail, through one mountain valley after another. Operated as a part of North Bend State Park, this trail has 10 tunnels and 37 trestles. There are several points of interest, including New Fort Salem at Salem, the Old Stone House at Pennsboro, and the glass industry in Ellenboro where marbles and hand-blown glassware are made. Ritchie County is famous for its asphalt mines which produced the material for many of Europe's first paved roads. Remnants of gas and oil fields dot the way.

At Parkersburg, a side-trip to Blennerhassett Island Historical State Park by stern-wheeler is worthwhile. Harman Blennerhassett built a mansion here in 1800 and allegedly plotted with Aaron Burr to establish an independent southwest empire. The ADT enters Ohio by crossing the U.S. 50 bridge over the Ohio River to Belpre.

Model section dedication at Smithburg on the North Bend Rail-Trail, West Virginia. North Bend Rail-Trail Foundation.

Ohio/Kentucky

The American Discovery Trail follows the blue-blazed Buckeye Trail for most of its route through Ohio from Chester Hill to Eden Park in Cincinnati. The 1,200-mile Buckeye Trail is unique among trails because it is the only trail that completely circles the state through which it runs. Co-aligned with the Buckeye Trail is the North Country National Scenic Trail. In 1803, Ohio was the first state to be carved out of the Northwest Territory. The Europeans who settled this region found hardwood forests that covered 95 percent of the land. Much of southern Ohio through which the ADT runs is still heavily wooded. The Appalachian Plateau in eastern Ohio has narrow valleys, steep hills, and many caves.

The ADT crosses the Ohio River into Belpre, passing through Blennerhassett Park and takes little-used back roads past Veto Lake to Vincent, Layman, and Chester Hill, where it joins the Buckeye

Downtown Cincinnati from Devoe Park, Covington, Kentucky. Reese Lukei, Jr.

Cedar Falls in Hocking Hills State Park, Ohio. Reese Lukei, Jr.

Trail. Following paved and gravel roads, the ADT passes through the southern part of Wolf Creek State Wildlife Area, around Burr Oak Reservoir in Burr Oak State Park to Tom Jenkins Dam and then into Wayne National Forest, which was named for Revolutionary War hero General Anthony Wayne. The trail traverses Trimble State Wildlife Area and re-enters Wayne National Forest on some of its 200 miles of trails, passing Lake Tecumsey south of the town of Shawnee.

The ADT passes through Webb Summit and enters the region of the Hocking Hills, an area of Black Hand sandstone hills, cliffs, and caves. This area of eroding sandstone was formed during the late Mississippian period when this was the shore of an ancient sea. Passing north of the town of Logan, the ADT connects the Cedar Falls, Old Man's Cave, and Ash Cave units of Hocking Hills State Park.

The route heads southwest through Tar Hollow State Forest east of Chillicothe, Ohio's first state capital, and on to Scioto Trail State Park and State Forest and the towns of Alma, Denver, and Nipgen, and Pike Lake State Park and State Forest. Near Sinking Spring, the ADT follows trails through Fort Hill State Memorial and Nature Preserve, the site of a prehistoric earthwork enclosing 48 acres believed to have been built by the Hopewell Indians. Now heading south, the trail passes the entrance to Serpent Mound Historic Site, the largest and finest serpent effigy in North America, and enters the community of Marble Furnace. Near Marble Furnace, the trail passes Wickerham Tavern, a historic two-story house that was a stop for runaway slaves on the Underground Railroad.

Davis Memorial Nature Preserve is 88 acres of rugged dolomite cliffs and rock towers northeast of West Union that the ADT passes through before circling the east side of Mineral Springs Lake. This part of Ohio is known as the "Little Smokies" because of its resemblance to the Great Smokies. The hills are steep, but the scale is smaller. Near Bentonville, after crossing a corner of Shawnee State Forest, the ADT passes the Counterfeit House built in 1840. It overlooks the Ohio River and was used to signal boat captains about the availability of counterfeit coins and bills. The house has false rooms, secret closets, and chimneys without fireplaces.

Heading northwest away from the Ohio River on gravel roads, the ADT crosses beautiful Eagle Creek Covered Bridge, built in 1872, and passes east of Georgetown to the small town of New Hope. The ADT goes along Grant Lake near Mount Orab, then over

Ohio coordinator Paul Daniel at the Buckeye Trail, Eden Park, Cincinnati. Reese Lukei, Jr.

the East Fork of the Little Miami River into Williamsburg. Eight miles of the Buckeye Trail are in East Fork State Park with its 2,160-acre lake. After going through the small town of Batavia, the ADT enters Milford, a suburb of Cincinnati, and the trail takes on a definite urban character after going under I-275. From Milford to Krugerhill, the ADT follows an abandoned railbed along the Little Miami River.

The town of Mariemont is a planned community founded in 1923 and is on the National Register of Historic Places. From the village of Fairfax, the ADT is mostly on sidewalks into Eden Park where it leaves the Buckeye Trail. Eden Park offers splendid views from high above the Ohio River which allow you to see well into Kentucky. On sidewalks through Mount Adams, a historic part of Cincinnati, the ADT heads downhill to the Riverwalk on the Bicentennial Commons. The South Western Ohio Trails Association has mounted a bronze plaque at Yeatman's Cove recognizing that the American Discovery Trail comes through Cincinnati. The ADT passes the famous statue of the *Flying Pigs* and Riverfront Stadium

Anderson Ferry, Ohio River, Ohio. Reese Lukei, Jr.

Farm road in Ohio. Reese Lukei, Jr.

and crosses the Roebling Suspension Bridge into Covington, Kentucky.

Covington experienced a major influx of German immigrants in the 1840s and their history and settlement is preserved in an area known as MainStrasse. A steep climb up a set of cement steps takes the ADT to Devou Park where there are outstanding views of Covington and downtown Cincinnati. After crossing the Ohio River (for the third time) on the historic Anderson Ferry, the ADT is back in Ohio. The trail passes the tomb of President William Henry Harrison as it follows close to the Ohio River.

The Southern Midwest Route of the ADT enters Indiana on State Line Road. The Northern Midwest Route of the ADT turns north, to Miami Whitewater Forest, passing near Okeana into Reily. On this route the ADT passes the Governor Bebb Preserve, Bunker Hill Haven for Boys, and Indian Creek Preserve. Oxford is the home of Miami University, founded in 1809. In Hueston Woods State Park the ADT takes the West Shore, Sugar Bush, Big Woods, and Hedge Apple trails. Continuing north the trail is on little-used country roads, going through Fairhaven and over the Harshman Covered Bridge to Concord Church. The Northern Midwest Route of the ADT enters Indiana east of Richmond on Druly Road.

Indiana

Indiana, the smallest state west of the Appalachian Mountains except for Hawaii, is known as the "Crossroads of America" because of its central location. The Northern Midwest Route of the ADT goes northwest from Richmond across the great Midwestern Corn Belt to the more industrialized region south of Gary. The Southern Midwest Route of the ADT follows along and just north of the Ohio River through the Southern Hills region which was the only part of Indiana that glaciers did not reach. As with other midwestern states, La Salle was the first European explorer to reach the area in 1679. France surrendered the region to Great Britain in 1763 after the French and Indian War. Indiana became a territory (including what is now Illinois, Wisconsin, and parts of Michigan and Minnesota) in 1800, and the nineteenth state in 1816.

View from Round Knob on the Knobstone Trail, Indiana. Indiana Department of Natural Resources.

Northern Midwest Route

The Northern Midwest Route of the ADT enters Indiana from Ohio on Druly Road, east of Richmond, then follows back roads until joining the Whitewater Valley Gorge National Recreation Trail at Test Road in Richmond. This 3½-mile trail has nine bridges and passes through nearly vertical cliffs of 500-million-year-old limestone in which are embedded one of the world's best fossil records of primitive animals that lived here when this area was a shallow inland sea.

After passing Thistlethwaite Falls, the ADT proceeds into Marion on the developing Cardinal Greenway, a rail-trail project under the leadership of the Landscape Architecture Department of Ball State University in Muncie. This trail is named for the Cardinal, one of the last passenger trains to travel this Cincinnati to Chicago route.

The ADT leaves the Cardinal Greenway in Marion and follows the river walk along the Mississinewa River in Marion. Back roads then lead to Frances Slocum State Recreation Area. Frances Slocum was a white woman captured on the frontier in Pennsylvania and adopted into the Miami tribe. The trail passes through Peru, the home of Cole Porter and the former winter grounds of several circuses. Back roads connect Lake Manitou near Rochester to Tippecanoe River State Park, Jasper-Pulaski State Fish and Wildlife Area, and La Salle State Wildlife Area. Jasper-Pulaski provides the opportunity to observe large numbers of sandhill cranes as they rest during their spring and fall migrations. The ADT leaves Indiana on Indiana 10 just south of La Salle State Fish and Wildlife Area and the Kankakee River.

Southern Midwest Route

The Southern Midwest Route of the ADT enters Indiana on paved State Line Road and follows roads through Greendale and into Lawrenceburg, an early 1800s steamboat town on a bend in the Ohio River. Aurora, known as "River City U.S.A.," is on Indiana 56 which turns west away from the Ohio River. Parts of the route into Farmers Retreat are on gravel roads and pass through the small towns of Hartford and Milton. This section is known as the Laugherty Creek Trail and is an official Boy Scout trail, although it is on paved and gravel roads. Friendship is the site of the annual National Muzzle-Loading Rifle Association competition. Following Indiana 62 (which is the Chief White Eye Trail, an Indiana

Lincoln Boyhood Home in Indiana. Reese Lukei, Jr.

A round barn near Muncie along the Cardinal Greenway. Reese Lukei, Jr.

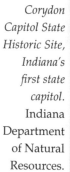

Corydon Capitol State Historic Site, Indiana's first state capitol. Indiana Department of Natural Resources.

Thistlethwaite Falls on the Whitewater Valley Gorge Trail in Richmond, Indiana. Reese Lukei, Jr.

scenic byway) through Cross Plains, Canaan, China, and Manville to Madison, brings the trail back to the Ohio River. The ADT passes through Clifty Falls State Park on trails and then the campus of Hanover College in Hanover.

Leave the Ohio River again and pass through Saluda, Chelsea, Lexington, and Underwood before reaching Clark State Forest. The Knobstone Trail follows 58 miles of the north-south Knobstone Escarpment. Travelers along the ADT will find that southern Indiana is quite hilly. The ADT joins the Knobstone Trail in Clark State Forest and goes south to the Deam Lake trailhead. From here, the ADT takes back roads through Wilson, Bennettsville, and St. Joseph into New Albany on the Ohio River across from Louisville, Kentucky. A greenway project under construction here will be the location of the ADT when it is completed. In nearby Jeffersonville guided tours are available at Hillerich & Bradsby Company, makers of the Louisville Slugger baseball bat.

The ADT follows Indiana 111 south along the river to Bridgeport then turns west through New Middleton to Corydon, the first state capital of Indiana in 1816. Corydon was the site of Indiana's only

Civil War battle. The ADT joins the 27-mile Adventure National Recreation Trail in Harrison-Crawford State Forest which is maintained by the Southern Indiana Hiking Club. Wyandotte Caves are nearby; they were used by prehistoric Indians and have the largest helictite formations of their type in the world.

The ADT again winds high above the Ohio River with great views, passing through Leavenworth, Fredonia, Alton, and Dexter before entering Hoosier National Forest. Through the Hoosier the ADT is on the Mogan Ridge, Tipsaw Lake, and Two Lakes trails.

The ADT is on a gravel road from Sassafras through Adyeville to St. Meinrad. The route then passes through Fulda and on to Santa Claus, where the Holiday World amusement park is located. Lincoln Boyhood National Memorial preserves the farm where Abraham Lincoln lived from 1816–30. The ADT enters Lincoln State Park, where on summer evenings the musical drama *Young Abe Lincoln* can be enjoyed.

The Big Bend of the Ohio River near Leavenworth, Indiana. Ron Craig.

Clifty Falls, Clifty Falls State Park, Madison, Indiana. Indiana Department of Natural Resources.

The ADT is on gravel roads from Gentryville through Folsomville to Boonville, where a visit to the Warrick County Museum is recommended. On gravel roads, the ADT heads south through Pelzer to Indiana 662 (Hoosier Heritage Scenic Trail) near Newburg where the ADT is once again along the Ohio River. This part of Indiana has many strip coal mines. Angel Mounds State Historic Site is the location of the largest and best preserved prehistoric Indian Mounds dating from 1200 to 1400.

The ADT through Evansville takes Memorial Parkway which is a greenbelt along which there are historic monuments and the Evansville Museum of Arts and Sciences. After leaving Evansville, the ADT is on gravel roads through Heusler to Mount Vernon and then Hovey Lake, which has a cypress swamp. The ADT crosses the Wabash River on Indiana 62 into Illinois.

Illinois

Illinois, the Prairie State, is mostly a land that glaciers have smoothed out and left with rich deposits of soil that produce abundant crops. Under that soil lies the largest coal reserves in the nation, but it is manufacturing that provides the most employment. French explorers Jolliet and Marquette traversed Illinois in 1673, and the first permanent European settlement was established at Cahokia by French priests in 1699. The British took title to Illinois in 1763 after the French and Indian War. Illinois became a Virginia county in 1778, part of the Northwest Territory in 1787, and the twenty-first state in 1818.

Lock on the Hennipen Canal, which connects the Illinois and Mississippi rivers. Reese Lukei, Jr.

The ADT's two routes through Illinois are quite different in character. The Northern Midwest Route is across land that is flat to slightly undulating mostly along two canals. By contrast, the Southern Midwest Route goes through very hilly country, untouched by glaciers. This area is known as the Illinois Ozarks or the Shawnee Hills and geologically remains much as it has been for eons.

Northern Midwest Route

The Northern Midwest Route of the ADT enters Illinois on Illinois 114 and follows back roads north to Western Avenue in Park Forest where it joins the Old Plank Road Trail, a 20-mile rail-trail project. The Old Plank Road was originally an Indian trail, then a

Fall colors at Garden of the Gods, a scenic national natural landmark in southern Illinois. Ray Morris.

wooden (plank) road that was followed by pioneers, and until 1976, an active railroad. It is now being converted back into a trail and will extend through Matteson, Rich Township, Frankfort, New Lenox, and into Joliet. In Joliet the ADT joins the Illinois and Michigan Canal State Trail for the next 70 miles to LaSalle.

In 1984, Congress established the Illinois and Michigan Canal National Heritage Corridor in recognition of the national significance of the historic Illinois and Michigan Canal and the surrounding landmarks, communities, and transportation networks. The 97-mile I & M Canal was built between 1836 and 1848 and was the first of the man-made waterways that established the corridor as a transportation network connecting the Gulf of Mexico by way of the Mississippi River to the Atlantic Ocean by way of the Great Lakes and the St. Lawrence Seaway.

The I & M Canal State Trail uses what was once the towpath along the canal, which was dug just north of the Illinois River. The trail begins south of Joliet and passes through Channahon, McKinley Woods, and William G. Stratton state parks, and Gebhard Woods State Park in Morris. The biggest tree in Illinois, an eastern cottonwood, grows in Gebhard Woods. Continuing west the trail connects Senaca, Marseilles, Ottowa, Utica, and LaSalle. Near Utica is Starved Rock and Matthiessen state parks.

The 16-mile section between LaSalle and Bureau, where the Hennepin Canal begins, is currently on back roads, but an effort is underway to build the Kaskaskia Trail which will connect the I & M with the Hennepin Canal as part of the plan to develop a much larger regional trail known as the Grand Illinois Trail. The 104-mile Hennepin Canal was hand-dug from 1890 to 1907 to connect the Illinois River to the Upper Mississippi River Valley and was in operation until 1951. It provided a direct water route between Chicago and the Mississippi River. Operated as a state park, the Hennepin Canal begins in Bureau and passes through Tiskilwa, Wyanet, Sheffield, Mineral, Annawan, Atkinson, and north of Geneseo to Green Rock. There are 32 locks on the Hennepin Canal that raise or lower the water level a total of 289 feet. The ADT continues on back roads to Hampton on the Mississippi River where it becomes part of the developing Great River Trail through East Moline, Moline, and the U.S. Army Rock Island Arsenal before crossing the Mississippi River into Davenport, Iowa, on the Government Bridge.

Southern Midwest Route

The Southern Midwest Route of the ADT crosses the Wabash River into Illinois on Illinois 141 just north of where the Wabash empties into the Ohio River. Following back roads the trail passes through New Haven then turns south near Omaha on Illinois 1 and crosses the Saline River as it enters Shawnee National Forest.

The ADT becomes a part of the 146-mile River to River Trail just west of where it begins on the Ohio River at Battery Rock. Recently completed, the River to River Trail was designed, constructed, and marked in just four years by equestrian and hiking advocates of the River to River Trail Society in southern Illinois. They had great cooperation from the Shawnee National Forest through which the trail travels for most of its distance to Devil's Backbone Park on the Mississippi River at Grand Tower.

Proceeding west on the River to River Trail, the ADT is now in the rugged hills and mixed hardwoods of the Illinois Ozarks. Passing through Camp Cadiz, an old CCC camp, the trail is soon in the Garden of the Gods, an area of steep cliffs and huge eroded rocks which affords outstanding vistas of the surrounding hills. The trail passes through the community of Herod to One Horse Gap and on to Lusk Creek Canyon National Natural Landmark before reaching Eddyville. The trail passes Jackson Hole, Peter Cave, Crow Knob, and Sand Cave, the largest sandstone cave in North America, which may have been occupied by humans for about 12,000 years. Millstone Bluff is a National Register Site that was a Mississipian Indian village and a pioneer quarry from which they dug rock for their millstones.

At Cache Lake the River to River Trail crosses the proposed Tunnel Hill Rail-Trail. The trail enters Ferne Clyffe State Park which has many unique rock formations, including Hawks' Cave, a 150-foot-long shelter bluff. The I-57 crossing provides an overlook that allows one to see where the Illinois Ozarks and the area known as the Mississippi Delta meet. Giant City State Park offers an extensive trail system. During the Civil War both Union and Confederate soldiers used the park's rock shelters and canyons as havens. The River to River Trail goes around Cedar Lake and through the village of Pomona to Clear Springs Wilderness and LaRue Pine Hills. From Horseshoe Bend, a high bluff overlooking the Mississippi River, the River to River Trail descends to pass through Winters Pond and terminates at Grand Tower.

Tourists enjoy viewing the Popeye *statue, located just off the Chester Bridge over the Mississippi River in Chester, Illinois.* Reese Lukei, Jr.

The ADT continues north on a combination of back roads and maintenance roads on the top of the levees along the Mississippi River to south of East St. Louis. There are several historic sites along this portion of the ADT, including Fort Kaskaskia, founded by Jesuit priests in 1703 at the site of an Indian village; Fort de Chartres, built by the French in 1720; Modoc, where a rock shelter is said to be the site of the longest continuous habitation in North America; Prairie du Rocher, first settled in 1722 as a French trading post; and Cahokia, the oldest town in Illinois settled in 1699 by French priests who established a mission here. A statue of Popeye stands in Chester, home of the creator of the cartoon character. In St. Clair County the levee trail is known as the Metro-East Levee Trail, which is part of the regional Gateway Trailnet system of trails. The ADT crosses the Mississippi River into Missouri from south of East St. Louis on the Eads Bridge which will have a pedestrian walkway when completed in 1995.

Illinois and Michigan Canal Trail near Morris, Illinois. Reese Lukei, Jr.

The Pine Hills overlook the American Bottoms of the Mississippi Valley. Ray Morris.

Iowa

Iowa was landscaped during the Ice Age by four massive glaciers that smoothed out some of the hills and left perhaps the most fertile soil in the world. Farms take up about 90 percent of the gently rolling land that produces more corn and beans than any other state, as well as many other crops. Iowa is also the leading manufacturer of farm and road construction machinery. Jolliet and Marquette were the first European explorers to visit the state in 1673. The first settler was Julien Dubuque in 1788, when he received permission from the Fox Indians to mine lead on their land in what is now the city of Dubuque. Iowa, which then included parts of present-day Minnesota and North and South Dakota, became a part of the United States in 1803 as part of the Louisiana Purchase and the twenty-ninth state in 1846. The state's nickname, the Hawkeye State, is said to honor Chief Black Hawk who led the Sauk and Fox tribes during the Black Hawk War of 1832.

The ADT enters Iowa at Davenport and begins its journey on one of the many rail-trail projects that has made Iowa a leader in the conversion of abandoned rail rights-of-way into recreational and non-highway transportation corridors. The route through downtown Davenport is on the Riverfront Trail which is partly on a rail-with-trail along the Mississippi River. This trail is also part of the proposed Great River Trail that one day could follow the entire length of the Mississippi River.

Leaving Davenport, the ADT temporarily follows Iowa 22 to Muscatine, a town in which Samuel Clemens lived and found inspiration for some of his writings. The ADT in Muscatine is on a newly constructed trail along the Mississippi River before turning west where it will eventually join the Hoover Nature Trail, a former Chicago, Rock Island, and Pacific rail line, at Conesville. Heading north through Nichols and West Liberty, the Hoover Nature Trail passes through West Branch, the birthplace of President Herbert Hoover and location of the Herbert Hoover Presidential Library and Museum.

Cedar Valley Nature Trail. Tom Neenan.

Continuing north the Hoover Nature Trail goes through Oasis, Morse, Solon, Ely, and into Cedar Rapids where the ADT is on its metro trail system, passing the National Czech and Slovak Museum and Library. Cedar Rapids is noted as the road building machinery capital of the world and the home of the world's largest cereal mill.

At Hiawatha, a suburb north of Cedar Rapids, the ADT joins the 52-mile Cedar Valley Nature Trail, one of our nation's first rail-trail projects. This limestone path following the Red Cedar River is well used by local residents. There are railroad depots at Center Point and Gilbertville that have been faithfully restored. An

Cedar Valley Nature Trail. Greg Kovaciny.

Mississippi River Trail, Muscatine, Iowa. Reese Lukei, Jr.

unusual feature of this trail is the opportunity to enjoy summer music concerts at Buzzard's Glory Quarry by walking or bicycling 3.5 miles from McFarlane Park. The northern end of the Cedar Valley Nature Trail is across from Deerwood Park in Evansdale. The Cedar Prairie Trail, a newly developing trail, will begin here and take the ADT into Waterloo where the Cedar Valley Lakes Trail and trails in George Wyth State Park become the route. The Waterloo/Cedar Falls metro area is the northernmost point on the ADT and where the ADT turns south along farm-to-market roads to Hudson and Voorhies and then west to Reinbeck.

From here through Morrison to Grundy Center the ADT is on the Pioneer Trail, another packed limestone rail-trail. Again on farm-to-market roads the ADT heads south to Beaman, then turns west and joins the Comet Trail to Conrad where back roads take the ADT into Marshalltown. The Heart of Iowa Nature Trail begins in Melborne and takes the ADT through Rhodes, Collins, Maxwell, Huxley, and into Slater. Near Madrid the ADT follows the Saylorville-Des

Old Depot Restaurant & Pub on the Raccoon River Valley Trail. Reese Lukei, Jr.

Moines River Trail south to Des Moines. Much of this trail is maintained by the U.S. Army Corps of Engineers. Des Moines is the capital of Iowa and the world's third largest insurance center where some sixty firms have corporate headquarters. The trail passes near Living History Farms, a 600-acre open-air agricultural museum that tells the story of farming in the Midwest from a 1700s Iowa Indian village to a modern crop center.

West of Des Moines at Clive, the ADT becomes part of the Raccoon River Valley Trail and passes through Waukee, Adel, Redfield, Linden, and Panora to Herndon. This trail winds through prairie remnants and bottomland timber areas. Adel has a beautifully restored railroad depot which is a restaurant. From Herndon the ADT will eventually follow a developing rail-trail that as yet has not been named. It will temporarily be on county roads through the communities of Coon Rapids, Dedham, and Templeton then south on a former railroad right-of-way through Audubon and Atlantic into Council Bluffs. Plans call for the National Park Service National Trail Center to be located here.

Cedar Valley Nature Trail, Iowa. Reese Lukei, Jr.

Lake McConaughy. Nebraska Game and Park Commission.

Nebraska

Nebraska certainly deserves to be known as the "Historic Trails" state. The Lewis and Clark, Mormon Pioneer, Pony Express, Oregon, and California national historic trails all cross Nebraska. Other non-designated trails such as the Overland, Oxbow, Texas-Ogalalla Cattle, and Nebraska City Cut-Off trails once laced the countryside. The Platte River, along which many of the trails run, is the source of the name Nebraska, which in the Oto Indian language means "flat water." Most who rushed across the state to get to the California gold fields or to their land of promise, failed to realize the riches that Nebraska held in its soil. With excellent soil conditions and plentiful water from the Missouri, Platte, and Niobrara rivers, Nebraska, for those who stayed, was the "promised land." Corn is Nebraska's number one agricultural crop, thus giving the state its "Cornhusker" nickname.

Sandhill cranes at Rowe Sanctuary on the Platte River. Nebraska Game and Parks Commission.

MoPac East Trail, Walton, Nebraska. Susan Rodenburg.

The ADT currently enters Nebraska by crossing the Missouri River on the South Omaha Bridge. The Lewis and Clark National Historic Trail follows the Missouri River from the Mississippi River. The Omaha-Metropolitan Area Trails Plan, a ten-year trails development plan, will present several options for improving the route through Omaha. The preferred route would cross the Missouri River on a new pedestrian bridge near Omaha's downtown. It will follow a riverfront trail to Haworth Park in Bellevue, Nebraska's oldest community. From there, it will use the Bellevue Loop, Papio, West Papio, and 144th Street trails. Omaha is Nebraska's largest city and the birthplace of President Gerald Ford, Malcolm X, and Marlon Brando. Boys Town, the Henry Doorly Zoo, and Joslyn Art Museum are located here.

The ADT will follow a trail parallel to Nebraska 50 to Wabash and the MoPac East Trail into Lincoln. A stop midway along the MoPac East Trail in Walton at the Walton Trail Company is recommended. ADT Nebraska Coordinator Susan Rodenburg is a co-owner.

Lincoln is the capital of Nebraska, the only state to have a one-house (unicameral) legislature. The Museum of Nebraska History houses three floors of exhibits from prehistoric times to the present.

The ADT follows paved and dirt roads from Lincoln to Central City, passing through or near Malcolm, Valparaiso, Dwight, Brainard, David City, Shelby, Osceola, Stromsburg, Polk, and Hordville. There are two rail-trail projects in this area that will take the ADT off-road in the future. One project is the Bohemian Alps Trail between Valparaiso and Brainard. At Central City the ADT meets the Platte River and the Oregon National Historic Trail, which is on the south side of the river.

The ADT continues on country roads to Grand Island and crosses under I-80 to Doniphan. The Stuhr Museum of the Prairie Pioneer in Grand Island has an exhibit on pioneer life and a reconstructed rail-road town of the 1860s. The route stays mostly on dirt roads south of the Platte River through Denman, Lowell, and Newark to Fort Kearney State Historical Park, a government outpost established in 1848. In the ensuing years, it protected pioneers on the Oregon Trail, crews building the Union Pacific Railroad, and mail-carrying stage-coaches. The broad flat Platte River Valley is the site of one of the wonders of the natural world as nearly 500,000 sandhill cranes gather here from late February through early April on their spring migration northward. The Pony Express National Historic Trail joined the Great Platte River Road with the Oregon Trail, and the Mormon Pioneer National Historic Trail began following this route on the north side of the Platte River at Grand Island.

Buffalo Bill Home, North Platte, Nebraska. Reese Lukei, Jr.

From Johnson Lake State Recreation Area near Lexington the ADT follows maintenance roads along the Tri-County Supply Canal to south of North Platte. These maintenance roads are currently restricted to maintenance vehicles and foot traffic only. Towns along this section include Cozad, the location of the Robert Henri Museum, and Gothenburg, the site of a Pony Express station and the Sod House Museum. The Fort McPherson National Cemetery is west of Jeffrey Reservoir. Buffalo Bill's Ranch State Historical Park is located in North Platte.

From Lake Maloney State Recreation Area continue following the canal road system to the north shore of Sutherland Reservoir where the ADT passes north of I-80 and follows the Sutherland and Keith-Lincoln County canals to Lake McConaughy north of Ogallala. Near the west end of the lake, the trail enters Ash Hollow State Historical Park which lies on an unusual geologic stratum known as the Ash Hollow formation. This is an excellent example of the landscape of the central Great Plains just before the Ice Age. Deep ruts of the Oregon Trail can be seen at Windlass Hill. The ADT heads south on county roads to Big Springs and enters Colorado near Julesburg and the intersection of Interstates 76 and 80.

Oregon Trail at Ash Hollow State Historical Park, Nebraska. Reese Lukei, Jr.

Missouri

Missouri, the Show Me State, was first claimed by the French explorer La Salle for France in 1682. By 1762, France had given the region, which La Salle had named "Louisiana," to Spain, but in 1800 Napoleon forced Spain to return the land to France. The United States acquired the land in 1803 as part of the Louisiana Purchase, and in 1812 Congress formed most of what had been called Upper Louisiana into the Missouri Territory. Lewis and Clark began their historic expedition where the Missouri River empties into the Mississippi River just north of St. Louis. The ADT follows their route along the Missouri River from St. Charles to Boonville on the Katy Trail.

The route of the ADT from Boonville to Kansas City is expected to change in the future as the result of efforts to develop a new rail-trail from Boonville through Sedalia, Windsor, Post Oak, Medford, Pleasant Hill, and into Kansas City. This relocation will likely not be completed for several years, and the route described in this guide, which follows the Santa Fe Trail from its origin near Boonville, should be used until then.

After crossing the Mississippi River into St. Louis on the Eads Bridge with its new pedestrian walkway, the ADT immediately enters the Jefferson National Expansion Memorial, which houses the Museum of Westward Expansion and is the site of the 630-foot-high Gateway Arch. The route then follows city sidewalks in an urban environment to Forest Park and crosses the Missouri River on the Discovery Bridge at St. Charles. Originally known as Les Petites Côtes (the little hills) by the French, then San Carlos by the Spanish, the town became St. Charles in 1804.

The ADT joins the 250-mile Katy Trail here. It follows the north bank of the Missouri River to Franklin, then crosses the river at Boonville, and goes cross-country to Clinton. This was the route of the Missouri-Kansas-Texas (MKT) Railroad which was built in the 1870s and was affectionately known as "the Katy." It ceased operations in 1986. The Katy Trail is administered as a Missouri State Park and begins northeast of St. Charles at Machens. The ADT joins the Katy in Frontier Park in St. Charles. Heading west from St.

Katy Trail on the ADT in Missouri near Rocheport, Missouri. Reese Lukei, Jr.

Charles, the Katy passes limestone bluffs in the Weldon Springs Wildlife Area. The trail is ideal for bird watching as it is located along the Missouri River flyway which is used by many migrating songbirds and waterfowl. Daniel Boone lived the last twenty years of his life near Defiance, and his four-story Georgian-style home, built between 1803 and 1810, is open to visitors.

Many Germans settled in this area and during the nineteenth century it became known as the "Missouri Rhineland." Many wineries are located along or near the trail between St. Charles and Rocheport. Bluffs appear again near Augusta, this time composed of dolomite and sandstone. In Dutzow and Marthasville, ornately stamped metal fronts on store buildings reflect the industrial age brought by the railroad. In Hermann, across the Missouri River from the Katy Trail, several wineries offer samples of their wine, cheese, and sausage, and the Hermann Museum, housed in the 1871 German School Building, has displays on steamboats and river history.

The ADT passes north of Jefferson City, the capital of Missouri. Towering limestone and dolomite bluffs border the trail from here to Rocheport. These bluffs were sacred to the Indians who called them the Manitou (Great Spirit) Bluffs. American bald eagles are common along this section in winter. Hartsburg, McBaine, and Huntsdale are typical post-Civil War railroad towns. A spur of the MKT has been converted into a rail-trail that goes into downtown Columbia and the University of Missouri-Columbia. Rocheport prospered as a riverboat town before the Civil War, and a large part of the town is listed on the National Register of Historic Places. The railroad tunnel just west of Rocheport is the only tunnel on the Katy Trail.

Franklin and then Boonville were where the first great wagon trains started out on the Santa Fe Trail. The first battle of the Civil War in Missouri was fought at Boonville. Boone's Lick State Historic Site is nearby. It comprises two salt springs where Daniel Boone's sons, Daniel and Nathan, made salt by heating brine in large iron pots. The route from Boonville to Kansas City is on gravel and paved roads, and as mentioned above is intended to be only a temporary route for the ADT.

Arrow Rock was a thriving Santa Fe Trail town, which today is preserved as Arrow Rock State Historic Site. The ADT leaves the Missouri River and follows the historic Santa Fe Trail as closely as

possible. It takes gravel roads north of Marshall and on to Waverly. From here the ADT is on the shoulder of paved roads into Kansas City, staying south of the Missouri River.

In Lexington the ADT passes the Battle of Lexington State Historic Site where a Civil War conflict known as the Battle of the Hemp Bales was waged. The battle was so named because Confederate soldiers used hemp bales as movable breastworks. Entering Jackson County the route is marked with Lewis and Clark Trail Motor Route signs. The terrain through this region is rolling hills. Near Sibley is Fort Osage, the first U.S. outpost in the Louisiana Purchase, which has been restored and is open to the public. The route passes the entrance to River Bluff Nature Preserve and Vaile Mansion, a thirty-room 1880s home described at the time as "the most princely house and the most comfortable home in the entire west."

The ADT follows a trail along the Blue River passing through three Jackson County Recreation areas. Enter Independence and pass the Bingham-Waggoner Estate. The route through Independence follows the signs for the Old Santa Fe Trail to Swope Park in Kansas City. Independence is the home of President Harry S. Truman, and his home, library, and museum are open daily. The National Frontier Trails Center with displays on many of the frontier trails is also located here. The Independence and Kansas City route is entirely urban and is on city sidewalks for the most part. The ADT crosses into Kansas on Kenneth Road, which becomes 151st Street in Kansas, over a wooden bridge spanning the Blue River.

Gateway Arch, St. Louis, Missouri. Reese Lukei, Jr.

Fort Larned National Historic Site, along the Santa Fe Trail at Larned, Kansas. American Images.

Kansas

The American Discovery Trail through Kansas is 574 miles long and begins in Johnson County on its eastern border by crossing the Blue River on a wooden plank bridge on the outskirts of Leawood. The majority of the route through the Sunflower State is on paved or gravel back roads. About 28 miles of the route in Johnson County is on paved bike trails. There is a rail to trail effort in progress that holds some potential for moving about 35 miles of the ADT between Osage City and Council Grove onto trail in the future, with a possible extension to Herington.

Biking/hiking paths take the ADT through residential neighborhoods and office parks in Johnson County, which is Kansas City's premier suburban area. Reese Lukei, Jr.

After crossing into Kansas the route through the metropolitan area is on a combination of low volume roads, some with sidewalks, and a developing system of trails in Leawood, Overland Park, Lenexa, and Shawnee. One interesting part of this route is Corporate Woods, where the trail winds between the many buildings that make up the business park. Many of the people who work here walk or ride their bicycles from home. After passing Shawnee Mission Park, the trail stays south of the Kansas River and heads west through the towns of DeSoto, Clearview City, Eudora, and into Lawrence.

Both the Oregon and Santa Fe national historic trails pass through Douglas County. The ADT generally follows the route of the Santa Fe Trail for the remainder of the way west through Kansas. At Lawrence, the ADT goes through the campus of the University of Kansas and Clinton Lake State Park. This part of Kansas and the next 200 miles or so are anything but the flat image that most folks may have in their minds. The landscape in physiographic terms is known as Osage Questas, or hill-plains with rather steep slopes. Next are the Flint Hills where the bluestem pastureland varies from 100 to 400 feet in elevation. Then come the Smoky Hills which include Pawnee Rock, a famous Santa Fe Trail landmark.

The calaboose, which is where troublemakers in rowdy Dodge City were held, is preserved at the Boot Hill Museum. Reese Lukei, Jr.

This former depot at Council Grove may become part of a rail-to-trail development. Reese Lukei, Jr.

With a lot of ups and downs the ADT heads west on back roads through the communities of Richland, Overbrook, Burlingame, and into Council Grove. At one time Council Grove was the last and most important outfitting post on the Santa Fe Trail. There are twelve historic sites here, including the Madonna of the Trail, a sixteen-foot memorial to the courage of pioneer mothers, and the Old Kaw Mission and Museum. Continuing on back roads, the ADT traverses the Flint Hills, crosses the Cottonwood River near Durham, and enters McPherson where the first man-made diamond is on display in the McPherson Museum.

The landscape now begins to gain elevation slowly and the hills lessen as the ADT enters the Great Plains. Kansas usually produces more wheat than any other state and that fact becomes very evident to the ADT traveler. Not so evident are the salt mines that have been in operation since 1890 near Lyons. This land was occupied by the Quivira Indians and artifacts of their sixteenth-century culture are on exhibit in the Coronado-Quivira Museum.

At Great Bend the ADT joins the Arkansas River and follows it all the way to Cañon City, Colorado, about 500 miles west. The towering concrete grain elevators at Great Bend signal that this is the regional grain center. It was also the area's oil capital, and pumps still extract crude oil from underground reserves beneath the wheat fields. Fort Zarah was located here and guarded the Santa Fe Trail

These pintails are just one of over 250 species of waterfowl and shore birds—from whooping cranes to sandpipiers—migrating through the Cheyenne Bottom Wildlife Area, which was designated the first wetlands of international importance. Gene Brehm, Kansas Department of Wildlife and Parks.

until 1869. South of Great Bend is Quivira National Wildlife Refuge, a birder's paradise, where over 250 species of birds have been observed. The ADT goes north through Cheyenne Bottoms Wildlife Area, a 19,000-acre natural land sink that was once a favorite hunting ground for the Cheyenne Indians. Pawnee Rock State Historic Site was a prominent landmark on the Santa Fe Trail. The 100-foot-high red sandstone outcrop was the site of many Indian ambushes.

Larned is the midway point along the Santa Fe Trail. The Santa Fe Trail Center Museum and Cultural Center is located here. Also Fort Larned National Historic Site is one of the most complete preservations of western forts. Fort Larned was built in 1859 to protect the mail coaches and commercial wagon trains on the Santa Fe Trail. Further along the Arkansas River is Kinsley, once a railroad boom town, but today a quieter agricultural center. Kinsley is noted for being exactly halfway (by highway, not by trail) between San Francisco and New York City, 1,561 miles from either city.

Dodge City was fittingly called "Hell on the Plains" and the "Wickedest Little City in America." Its infamous Front Street was one of the wildest on the frontier, with a well-stocked saloon for every fifty residents. This is where cowboys, cattlemen, buffalo hunters, gunfighters, soldiers, and railroadmen all gathered to the delight of the brothelkeepers and morticians. Boot Hill got its name because so many men died with their boots on. There was a high-class side to Dodge City as well. In 1879 the Dodge City Cowboy Band, which performed at the Long Branch Saloon, gained national attention because of its good musicianship.

The ADT continues along the Arkansas River on mostly gravel roads to Cimarron where the Santa Fe Trail divides into the southern or Cimarron River route and the northern or mountain route. The mountain route, followed by the ADT, was developed in the 1840s because it provided more water sources than the usually dry Cimarron route.

Garden City is the center of one of the state's most intensively irrigated regions, producing bumper crops of wheat, corn, and alfalfa. A 4,000-acre state game preserve is home to a large herd of bison. Through Kearney County the ADT follows the River Road north of the Arkansas River. At Kendall the River Road goes south of the river through Hamilton County past Syracuse to the Colorado border near Coolidge. The route through Hamilton County was the first section of the ADT to be signed with ADT trail markers.

After a storm on the High Plains of Colorado. Reese Lukei, Jr.

Colorado

Colorado, the Centennial State, is the crossroads of many trails and many cultures. Ute Indians once roamed its mountains and Kiowa, Arapahoe, and Cheyenne camped in the cottonwood groves of its eastern plains. Spanish explorers from New Mexico probed its mountains and valleys in search of gold and silver. A rush of goldseekers with signs of "Pikes Peak or Bust" painted on their wagons descended on the region in 1859. Railroads, commerce, and permanent settlements quickly followed and Colorado joined the Union in 1876 as the thirty-eighth state. The mountain branch of the Santa Fe National Historic Trail crosses the state's southeastern corner, the Continental Divide National Scenic Trail runs the length of the state near the crest of its mountains, and the Colorado Trail connects Denver with Durango.

Trail dedication with Senator Hank Brown. Ron Ruhoff, Photomusical Adventures.

Northern Midwest Route

The Northern Midwest Route of the American Discovery Trail enters Colorado near Julesburg and follows the South Platte River Valley to the Denver suburb of Lakewood. This portion of the ADT is likely to change in the future because of the possibility of a rail-trail conversion and a planned National Wildlife Refuge. It is currently on back roads across the central high plains characterized by irrigated croplands and grazed grasslands.

Sterling is a ranching and agricultural center and headquarters for the oil and gas industry in northeast Colorado. The Overland Trail Museum and the Living Tree Sculptures, twenty larger-than-life wood carvings, including five giraffes, are located here. Fort Morgan was originally a military post and Overland Trail station, but is now a center of dairy farming and cattle ranching. The route through Denver follows the paved South Platte River Trail to its junction with the Bear Creek Greenbelt.

Southern Midwest Route

From the Kansas line near Holly to Cañon City, the Southern Midwest Route of the ADT climbs gradually across the eastern plains from 3,300 feet to 5,350 feet in about 160 miles. This route parallels the Arkansas River and the Santa Fe National Historic Trail on the shoulder of both paved and gravel roads through grasslands and several small ranching communities. La Junta, meaning "the junction" in Spanish, was the junction of the Santa Fe and old Navajo trails and is a major cattle and produce shipping center for the lower Arkansas Valley. Bent's Old Fort National Historic Site is 8 miles east of La Junta and was a major trading post on the Mountain Branch of the Santa Fe Trail. Kit Carson was employed at the fort as a hunter and scout. Comanche National Grassland is southwest of town.

Pueblo, another Spanish word meaning "town," is located on the site where in 1842 trader Jim Beckwourth constructed an adobe fortress at the confluence of the Arkansas River and Fountain Creek. Mountain men, traders, trappers, Indians, and immigrants convened at this crossroads which was the largest settlement in the region. Today, Pueblo is a major industrial center and the site of the Colorado State Fair. The Royal Gorge is located west of Cañon City and is spanned by the world's highest suspension bridge, 1,053 feet

The ADT skirts Pikes Peak, Colorado. Reese Lukei, Jr.

Roxborough State Park, Colorado. Reese Lukei, Jr.

above the Arkansas River. Between Cañon City and Salida, the Arkansas River offers many whitewater rafting opportunities.

From Cañon City the ADT follows the Shelf Ridge Road, a BLM backcountry byway, north to Cripple Creek. In about 40 miles the ADT gains over 4,100 feet and makes a grand entry into the Front Range of the Rocky Mountains. Cripple Creek is a National Historic Landmark District. In 1891, young Bob Womack found gold on his uncle's ranch. He rode to Colorado Springs to celebrate and sold his claim for $500, never dreaming that over $350 million in gold would eventually be extracted from his claim and others that were discovered nearby. Cripple Creek is one of the state's legalized gambling locations.

From Cripple Creek the ADT heads north over Ute Pass to Woodland Park and then north of Pikes Peak (14,110 feet) into Manitou Springs. A possible side trip is to take the 11-mile Barr National Recreation Trail to the top of Pikes Peak. From Manitou Springs the ADT travels past the Garden of the Gods, along Monument Creek, and through the U.S. Air Force Academy on the New Santa Fe Trail. Continuing north, the trail traverses the west side of Roxborough State Park and Pike National Forest on the east side of the Rampart Range before reaching Waterton Canyon and the start of the Colorado Trail. From the Chatfield State Recreation Area the ADT joins the Northern Midwest Route at the junction of the South Platte River and the Bear Creek Greenbelt.

The Bear Creek Greenbelt goes into Lakewood and then on to Morrison. Follow the Castle Trail at Mount Falcon Park to O'Fallon Park, then through downtown Evergreen to the People's Path to Elk Meadow. The ADT now enters the heart of the Rockies and the route becomes very rugged. Old Squaw Pass Road and Warren Gulch take the ADT past Mount Evans and into Idaho Springs. Spring Gulch and the Saxon Mountain Trail lead the ADT through an area around Clear and Chicago creeks where many gold and silver mines are located. From Georgetown the ADT enters Arapaho National Forest and follows the scenic byway over 11,669-foot Guanella Pass.

At Guanella Pass take the South Park Trail to Guanella Creek Road and Guanella Pass Road to Burning Bear Trail. Cross Hall Valley to Whale Peak and Glacier Peak in Pike National Forest. Join the Colorado Trail northeast of Georgia Pass and follow the Vail Pass Tenmile Canyon National Recreation Trail (co-located with the Colorado Trail) to Copper Mountain. Continue on the Tenth Mountain Division Trail System to Camp Hale and Tennessee Pass. During World War II, Camp Hale was the training center for America's famed mountain troops, the much-decorated Tenth Mountain Division. From Tennessee Pass follow U.S. 24 into Leadville, at 10,188 feet it's the highest town on the ADT. Leadville area mines have produced over $2 billion dollars worth of gold, silver, lead, and other minerals.

The ADT leaves Leadville on U.S. 24 and soon after crossing the Arkansas River joins the Colorado Trail and its alternate mountain bike route through Buena Vista to Mount Princeton Hot Springs, Cascade Campground, and St. Elmo in the San Isabel National Forest. Follow the Continental Divide National Scenic Trail over Tincup Pass and then the Timberline Trail south of the Collegiate Peaks Wilderness. Take dirt and four-wheel-drive roads to Taylor Pass. Follow Brush Creek down to Colorado 135 and into Crested Butte, a former coal mining town.

From Crested Butte the ADT goes north through Gothic and over Schofield Pass into the Gunnison National Forest to the Crystal River Jeep Trail, which runs between the Raggeds and the Maroon Bells-Snowmass wilderness areas. From the town of Redstone, the trail now follows Braderich Creek, Lake Ridge Lakes, Mid Thompson Park, and passes Haystack Mountain in the White River National Forest. The White River National Forest is home to one of the world's largest elk herds. The High Trail leads into Grand Mesa National Forest and the Sunlight-Powderhorn Snowmobile Trail. The Crag Crest National Recreation Trail, Kannah Creek Trail, and back roads take the ADT into the town of Whitewater.

From Whitewater, the ADT takes back roads south of Grand Junction to Colorado National Monument, where the trail follows the Liberty Cap, Black Ridge, and Monument Canyon trails. Future plans call for the ADT to be on the Colorado Riverfront Trail System in Grand Junction and on the Mesa Slope Trail. From Loma, northwest of Colorado National Monument, the ADT follows the Kokopelli Mountain Bike Trail into Utah.

Utah

Utah, the Beehive State, is a land of stark contrasts, and those following the route of the Discovery Trail will get to experience much of this variety. The eastern part is in red rock country on the Kokopelli Mountain Bike Trail along the Colorado River, and through the Canyonlands and Capitol Reef national parks. In central Utah the ADT traverses the heavily forested high mountains of the Dixie and Fishlake National Forests. The western part introduces the ADT traveler to very dry desert conditions that require careful planning for a safe journey.

Butch Cassidy Home, Circleville, Utah. Reese Lukei, Jr.

The American Discovery Trail enters Utah on the Kokopelli Mountain Bike Trail which begins at Loma, Colorado, and winds for 128 miles through desert sandstone and shale canyons until it reaches Moab, Utah. Most of the trail is on Bureau of Land Management land, but also goes briefly into the Manti-LaSal National Forest. Parts of this trail are quite steep and after a rain all parts of the trail can be difficult. The Kokopelli Trail crosses the Colorado River at Dewey. This is spectacular red rock country where many movies and television commercials have been filmed.

The ADT skirts Arches National Park with its more than 1,800 entrada sandstone arches, and the park is an easy side trip from Moab. The scenes in many of Zane Grey's novels were set in the Moab area, and Butch Cassidy's Wild Bunch and other outlaw gangs hung out here.

Capitol Reef National Park, Utah. Reese Lukei, Jr.

Waterpocket Fold in Capitol Reef National Park, Utah. Reese Lukei, Jr.

Leave Moab by way of the Kanes Creek Road, Hurrah Pass Trail, and Lockhart Basin Trail. The landscape is mostly sagebrush desert, but with towering cliffs above and along the Colorado River where it passes below Anticline Overlook. The trail enters Canyonlands National Park on Utah 211 and passes the Needles Visitor Center and Squaw Flat Campground. The Needles region of the park is a startling landscape of sculptured rock spires, arches, canyons, grabens, and potholes. The dominant land forms are the Needles themselves—naked rock pinnacles banded in orange and white. The ADT continues south through Chesler Park, a grassy meadow, and Beef Basin, a relatively flat 6,000-foot-high plateau. The ADT bypasses the Dark Canyon Wilderness on a jeep road through North Elk Ridge, South Elk Ridge, and Long Canyon on BLM and Manti-LaSal National Forest lands.

Red rock country in eastern Utah. Reese Lukei, Jr.

The Colorado River is crossed for the final time on the Hite Bridge on Utah 95 in Glen Canyon National Recreation Area. The ADT heads northwest on Utah 95 and near the junction of Utah 276 begins to climb into the Henry Mountains in Dixie National Forest, Utah's largest. The ADT passes between Mount Ellen (11,522 feet) and Mount Pennell (11,371 feet) on a combination of dirt roads and trails. The Henry Mountains are home to the only free-ranging buffalo herd in America. The ADT descends across Wildcat Mesa into Waterpocket Fold in Capitol Reef National Park. Here an alternate route can be followed south through Strike Valley along

Mineral Mountains near Beaver, Utah. Reese Lukei, Jr.

Notom-Bullfrog Road to the Burr Trail which ascends through the Waterpocket Fold to the town of Boulder, then north to rejoin the ADT at Roundup Flat on Utah 12. The Waterpocket Fold, created 65 million years ago, is a 100-mile-long nearly impassable ridge of vaulted white rock domes.

Climb out of Capitol Reef on the Oak Creek Trail to Utah 12 at Roundup Flat on Boulder Mountain. Looking back east, there are some great views of Capitol Reef and the Waterpocket Fold. The ADT joins the Great Western Trail in Dixie National Forest. From Boulder Mountain the ADT descends to the Aquarious Plateau and into the ranching community of Antimony. After crossing the Sevier Plateau the trail enters Circleville, the birthplace of Robert Leroy Parker, otherwise known as Butch Cassidy.

The climb out of Circleville is on the Paiute ATV Trail in the Fishlake National Forest and is quite steep. Circleville Mountain and the mountains around Beaver are home to mule deer and elk. Beaver is on the edge of the western Utah desert. Travel from here through the rest of Utah and most of Nevada must be carefully planned because of the lack of water and very few towns in which to resupply.

The ADT leaves Beaver, crossing over Soldier Pass in the Mineral Mountains and the Escalante Desert before arriving in Milford, the last town of any size that the ADT goes directly through until Virginia City, Nevada, over 500 miles west. From Milford the ADT is mostly on very seldom used dirt roads through the Wah Wah Valley, across snow-white Crystal Peak, and bone-dry Ferguson Desert. There is no source of water until reaching the small community of Garrison near the Nevada border.

Nevada

Nevada is a state of extremes. It has the least rainfall of any state, one of the smallest populations, and twenty-eight north-south mountain ranges that wrinkle the floor of the Great Basin. Its mines have produced vast amounts of silver, gold, and copper. Most of its rivers drain into "sinks" without outlets where the water evaporates, leaving alkali mud flats and dry lakes. Yet, it is one of the most visited of the fifty states, thanks to Reno and Las Vegas.

The name Nevada comes from a Spanish word meaning "snow-clad," and it is appropriate since some of the state's highest peaks can receive up to 225 inches of snow annually. Commonly known as the Silver State, Nevada is also nicknamed the Sagebrush State. It is the fourteen mountain ranges and the wide sagebrush-covered valleys in between them that the traveler along the American Discovery Trail will come to know and remember best.

Arc Dome, from the Toiyabe Crest National Recreation Trail, Nevada. Chris Macek.

The ADT in Nevada begins in Baker, a small community at the base of the Snake Range, which is the home of Great Basin National Park. The most prominent peak in the park is Wheeler Peak at 13,063 feet. Great Basin offers outstanding opportunities to hike in a variety of natural habitats ranging from sagebrush desert to alpine lakes. A bristlecone pine found here was determined to be the world's oldest living thing: 4,950 years old. Tours are given daily into the limestone and marble world of Lehman Caves with its stalactites, stalagmites, columns, flowstones, and its rare and mysterious structures called shields.

The ADT traverses the northern part of the park following Strawberry Creek uphill to where it crosses the remains of Osceola Ditch, which provided water to miners during the 1880s. The trail then heads downhill through Windy Canyon along Willard Creek,

Headwaters of the Reese River looking into the Arc Dome Wilderness, Indian Valley, Nevada. Chris Macek.

Great Basin National Park, Nevada. Reese Lukei, Jr.

passing through BLM lands and part of Humboldt National Forest (there was a forest fire here in 1994). From here you have a view of Spring Valley, the first of several wide sagebrush-covered valleys ahead of you, and the Schell Creek Range where the trail goes through Cooper Canyon to Cave Lake State Park. The 32-acre Cave Lake is noted for its brown trout. Ely, located 15 miles north via U.S. 6, is a major resupply point for trail travelers.

After crossing Steptoe Valley the route heads into the Egan Range, passing the Ward Charcoal Ovens State Historic Site where there are six massive beehive-shaped stone kilns built in 1876 to convert wood into charcoal for local mining smelters. The route across the Egan Range in Humboldt National Forest follows Water Canyon across the mountain into the White River Valley and the community of Preston. Here there are some supplies—a motel, gas station, and restaurant—outside of town on Nevada 318.

The White River Valley is wide and relatively flat, and, typical of nearly all of these valley crossings, the trail is on a seldom traveled

Remains of a mine building in Grantsville, Nevada. Reese Lukei, Jr.

dirt road. The White Pine Range is crossed on an old stagecoach road along Ellison Creek. The climb to the Ellison Ranger Station takes you through a canyon with sheer rock walls and the stone wall remains of a former stagecoach stop. After reaching the pass, you enter Freeland Canyon and descend through Blackrock Canyon to Bull Spring before entering Railroad Valley.

The Duckwater Shoshone Reservation is located here and is private property. The route of the ADT follows dirt roads south and west of the reservation and ADT travelers should observe the request of the residents to their right of privacy. This is the greenest valley you will see in Nevada. It is fed by many springs. The Pancake Range provides a rather gentle ascent and descent just south of Brown Summit.

Big Sand Springs Valley, like most of the land that is not national forest, is managed by the Bureau of Land Management. The dirt roads through this valley live up to their name—big sand. The gradual ascent into the Squaw Hills and the Confusion Hills is on a jeep road through Jumbled Rock Gulch into Hot Creek Valley and Moores Station (private property) which is a former stagecoach stop. There are a number of tall buttes and rock formations at this location. Hot Creek Valley is quite narrow. You soon begin to climb into the Hot Creek Range toward Morey Peak (10,246 feet). The ADT enters the Monitor Range on the Toiyabe National Forest and the Morey Peak and Fandango wilderness study areas where only foot and horse travel is permitted.

From Moores Station the climb is steep into Morey Canyon to Sixmile Summit near Mahogany Peak. The trail then proceeds to Cold Spring to Little Fandango to Upper Fish Lake to Little Fish Lake Valley. From the Little Fish Lake Valley ascend into the Table Mountain Wilderness through Green Monster Canyon to Mosquito Creek which descends into Monitor Valley. Look for elk which have been reintroduced on Table Mountain. Cross the sagebrush-covered valley to Pine Creek Campground and begin a moderate ascent into the Alta Toquima Wilderness in the Toquima Range. Pick up the Mount Jefferson Trail at South Summit and follow it north to Moores Creek Trailhead. The south summit of Mount Jefferson at 11,941 feet is a slight detour off the route. This is the highest point of the ADT in Nevada and the second highest peak in the state.

It is about 17 miles across Big Smoky Valley which is mostly BLM managed land. Arc Dome at 11,775 feet has been visible for several days and now it looms right above. The climb into the Arc Dome Wilderness begins at the South Twin Trailhead and follows the Toiyabe Crest National Recreation Trail across the mountain, south of Arc Dome, to the junction of Big Sawmill Creek and Little Sawmill Creek. Descend through Cow Canyon into the narrow and green Reese River Valley. The Yomba Shoshone Reservation is north of Grantsville Road where the ADT turns west, soon passing the ghost town of Grantsville. Several buildings in various stages of ruin remain as a reminder of better days when silver was mined here.

Nevada has preserved the ghost town of Berlin as a state park. Silver and gold were mined here from 1895 until 1911. Today, you can be guided through the town on regular weekend tours and learn about life as it used to be in Berlin. Berlin Ichthyosaur State Park preserves the fossil remains of the 50-foot "fish-lizard," Ichthyosaur, which lived here 225 million years ago when all this land was under water as a Mesozoic ocean.

In Ione, the town that refused to die (1994 population seven), you can picnic in a shaded park, refuel your car, get a meal, and down a cold beer at the Ore House Saloon & Restaurant. From Ione continue northwest on the dirt Ione Valley Road and cross Buffalo Summit in a pinyon and juniper forest. At Eastgate the road becomes paved and soon meets U.S. 50, "the loneliest road in America," which you follow west for 25 miles. For most of the way along this highway the old road is still there and usable as a trail, switching back and forth on either side of the current highway. You are now also following the route of the Pony Express National Historic Trail. There is a U.S. Navy Air Base near here and low-flying aircraft are regularly seen and heard. There is a store at Middlegate.

The ADT leaves the highway and cuts straight across the dry desert. Take plenty of water. Head west across the desert for Simpson Pass which is located between the Bunejug and Cocoon mountains. Continue across Wildcat Scarp south of the now dry Carson Lake (dry sink) and north of the White Throne Mountains. Pass the site of the Wildcat Freight Station on the Pony Express Trail. After crossing U.S. 95 where Fallon is 15 miles north, the route continues across the desert north of the Desert Mountains and south of the Dead Camel Mountains. These alkali flats are also called playa and should only be crossed when they are dry.

Fort Churchill was an important military garrison in the 1860s. The remains of the adobe buildings comprising the fort are a state

A stormy sky and ruins at Fort Churchill, Nevada. Steve Weaver.

Ruins of the Berlin Mill at the Berlin Townsite, Berlin Ichthyosaur State Park. Chris Macek.

historical park. The American Discovery Trail follows the Carson River from Fort Churchill to U.S. 50, where it leaves the Pony Express Trail. From there the route goes up Sixmile Canyon into Virginia City, home of the famous Comstock Lode and the liveliest ghost town in the west. Once an 1870s boomtown of 30,000 people and 110 saloons, today Virginia City has thousands of visitors and each September is host to the National Championship Camel Races. Mark Twain and Brett Hart honed their writing skills here as reporters for the *Territorial Enterprise*.

From Virginia City, the trail crosses Mount Davidson, through Washoe Lake State Park to the northern outskirts of Carson City, named in 1858 for Kit Carson. It was named the capital of Nevada when it became a state in 1864. From north of Carson City you begin a climb into the Sierra Nevada Mountains and to Tahoe Meadows. The ADT will be a part of the Tahoe Rim Trail that is in the process of being designed and constructed. The ADT continues in the Toiyabe National Forest north of Incline Village and into California.

Tahoe Meadows and the Tahoe Rim Trailhead near the Nevada-California border. Steve Weaver.

California

The American Discovery Trail enters California on the Tahoe Rim Trail in Tahoe National Forest on the eastern slopes of the Sierra Nevada Mountains. The exact route of some sections of the Tahoe Rim Trail has not yet been determined, but the ADT will follow the Rim Trail, when completed, into Squaw Valley. To the south, Lake Tahoe, called the "lake in the sky," is 22 miles long and 12 miles wide and has an average depth of 989 feet. The azure blue water is said to be 99.7 percent pure. To the north, Truckee was a rough-and-tumble lumber and railroad town during the gold rush days. Its false-front, nineteenth-century buildings remain as reminders of those days.

Limantour Beach at Point Reyes National Seashore, the western terminus of the ADT.
Reese Lukei, Jr.

Crossing the Golden Gate Bridge toward Marin County from San Francisco.
Reese Lukei, Jr.

The ADT crosses the 2,600-mile-long Pacific Crest National Scenic Trail just east of Granite Chief Peak in Tahoe National Forest. From Squaw Valley to Auburn, the ADT follows the Western States Trail, which each summer is the site of the 100-mile Western States Endurance Run and the Tevis Cup Ride for horses. This has been gold country since the days of the Forty-niners. The route follows the Middle Fork of the American River, past active placer gold mining operations which boast ample warnings about what can happen to claim jumpers. This section of the ADT drops from 8,700 feet at Emigrant Pass in the Sierras to 1,300 feet at Auburn. Along the way it passes places with names such as Last Chance, Dusty Corners, Devil's Thumb, Ruck-A-Chucky, and Deadwood Canyon and the small towns of Michigan Bluff and Foresthill before reaching Auburn.

Auburn claims the oldest continuously used post office in California, as well as the Gold Country Museum. The Jedediah Smith National Recreation and American River trails lead past Folsom Lake State Recreation Area and Captain John Sutter's grave to Sacramento, California's capital. In 1839, Sutter located a trading post at what became Sacramento. It is the western terminus of the Pony Express National Historic Trail and one of the termination points of the California National Historic Trail. The elevation here is about 30 feet and the city is a major inland port because of a deep-water channel to San Francisco Bay. Sacramento is the self-proclaimed "Camellia Capital of the World" and in March holds a ten-day Camellia Festival.

From Sacramento, the ADT traverses the flat region known as the Delta. This is an agricultural area with corn and wheat fields and fruit orchards. The trail passes through the towns of Freeport, Clarksburg, Hood, Courtland, Locke (a Chinese village dating to 1850), Walnut Grove, Ryde, and Isleton before reaching Antioch.

From Antioch to the Pacific Ocean, Contra Costa and Marin counties and the metropolitan Oakland and San Francisco areas are laced with a vast trail system. Leave Antioch on a bike path and cross the Contra Costa Canal twice before reaching Contra Loma Park. A series of trails (Stewartville, Miner's, Nortonville, Black Diamond, Donner Canyon, Bruce Lee, Mitchell Canyon, Deer Flat, Prospector's Gap, Devils Elbow, and North Peak) lead to the top of Mount Diablo, 3,849 feet high. From here, on a clear day you can see 600 miles of the Sierra Nevada Mountains and parts of thirty-five counties—more land area than from any other mountain in the world except Mount Kilimanjaro.

Another series of trails (Summit, Wall Point, Briones-Mount Diablo trails lead into Walnut Creek, then Contra Costa Canal, Acalanes Ridge, Lafayette Ridge, Homestead, Bear Creek, Old San Pablo, Inspiration Point, and part of the 400-mile Bay Area Ridge Trail) leads into Berkeley via Strawberry Canyon. Berkeley offers the highest concentration of espresso machines along any part of the ADT and the trail passes the campus of the University of California. In Jack London Square you board the Red & White Fleet ferry for a ride across San Francisco Bay to the Ferry Building on the Embarcadero in San Francisco. The Embarcadero takes the ADT past Fisherman's Wharf to Fort Mason Center. The Golden Gate Promenade through the Presidio takes the ADT to the Golden Gate Bridge. It is always windy on the bridge, so tie everything tightly onto your pack. The northern end of the Juan Bautista de Anza National Historic Trail is at the Presidio. Fort Point National Historic Site is located at the foot of the bridge on its southern side. Built by the U.S. Army in 1861, the fort is similar in design to that of Fort Sumter, South Carolina.

The ADT follows the Bay Area Ridge Trail via the Coastal, Miwok, Redwood Creek, and Dipsea trails through Marin County into Muir Woods National Monument. Muir Woods preserves one of the last remnants of the giant redwood trees that covered much of the Northern Hemisphere 140 million years ago. The mature coast redwoods here are between 500 and 1,000 years old and reach up to 250 feet in height. The ADT leaves Muir Woods on the Ben Johnson and Stapleveldt trails. The Bolinas Ridge, Randall, and Olema Valley trails reach Olema Valley and the San Andreas Rift Zone, where the ADT is within one mile of the epicenter of the 1906 earthquake.

The climb out of Olema Valley and into Point Reyes National Seashore is on the Stewart, Glen, Bear Valley, and Coast trails which bring the ADT to the Pacific Ocean. A short distance north along the shoreline is Limantour Beach and the western terminus of the American Discovery Trail. Congratulations! You made it!

California ADT coordinator John Fazel completing his 389-mile run of the ADT in California, June 3, 1993, on the Coast Trail, Point Reyes National Seashore, California. Reese Lukei, Jr.

Backpacker on the Knobstone Trail, Indiana. Ron Craig.

Appendices

Maps

The maps in this guide are based on a Trails Illustrated map of the entire American Discovery Trail. In addition to this overview map, Trails Illustrated is publishing the official American Discovery Trail map series consisting of nine regional maps. Each map shows the entire route for that particular region on one side and has detailed maps of key portions of the route on the other side. The regional maps will cover the following areas and be released throughout 1995 and early 1996.

California (available)
Delaware, Maryland, and eastern West Virginia
Western West Virginia, Ohio, Kentucky
Missouri, Illinois, and Indiana (the Southern Midwest Route)
Iowa, Illinois, and Indiana (the Northern Midwest Route)
Nebraska and Kansas
Colorado
Utah
Nevada

Trails Illustrated publishes a large selection of high quality national park and recreation maps. For further information, contact Trails Illustrated, P.O. Box 3610, Evergreen, Colorado 80439-3425; (800) 962-1643.

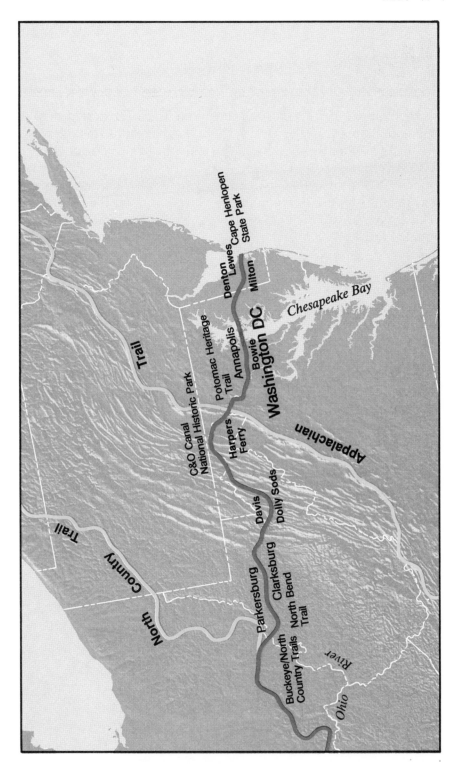

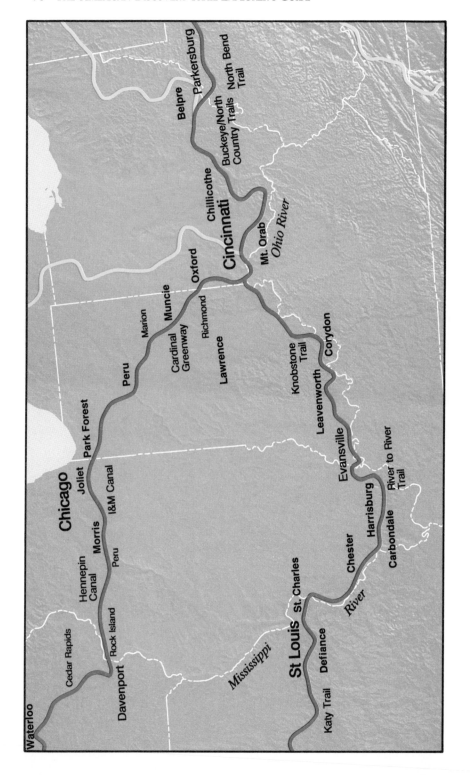

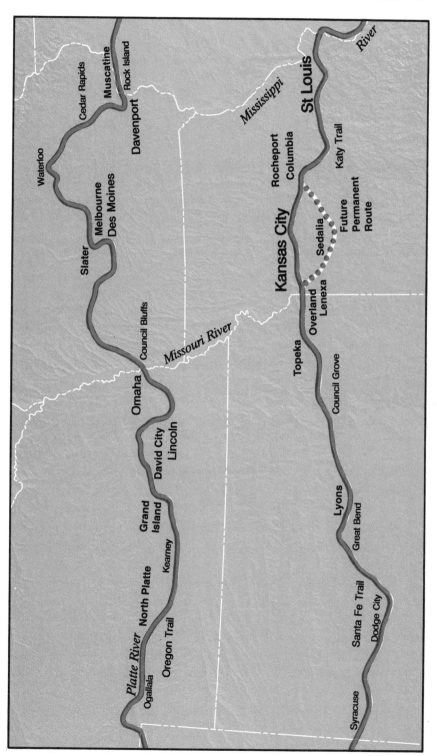

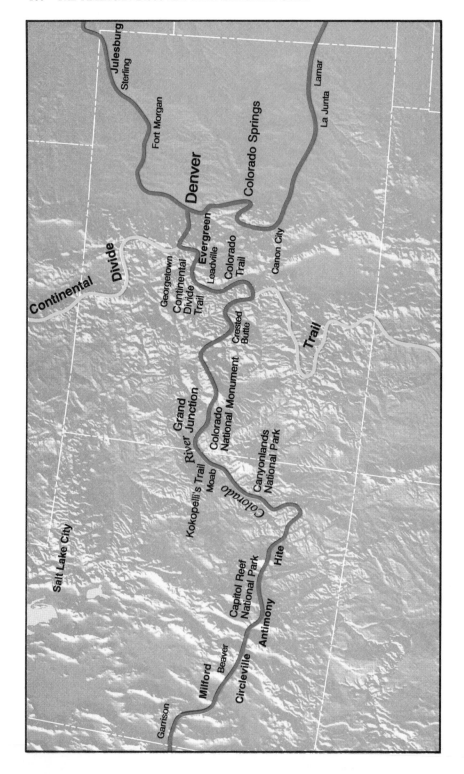

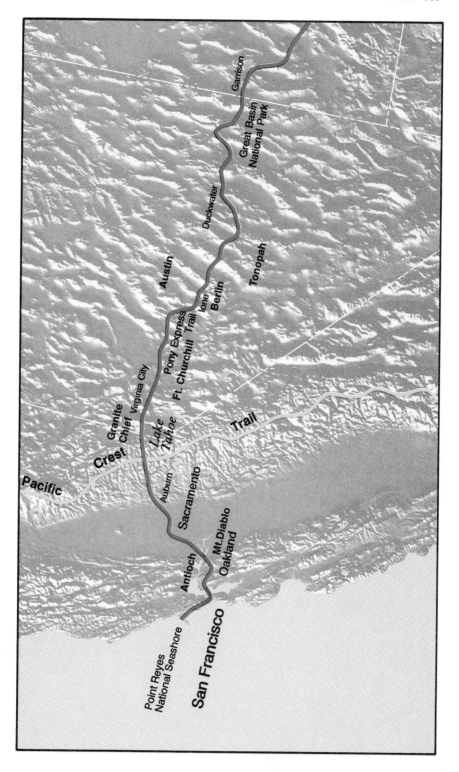

Mileage

Local Organizations
The Backbone of a Successful Trail

"A first-rate trails system can only be created by people."
— The Presidents' Commission
on Americans Outdoors

A word heard frequently in the trails community is "grassroots." It has certainly applied to the development of the American Discovery Trail. The ADT has been a "grassroots" project. The route location has been accomplished by people living in the areas through which the trail passes. Working with local, state, and federal land managers, local citizens have selected a route that provides the opportunity to see those special places that have been identified and protected as part of our natural, cultural, historic, and scenic heritage. The outstanding cooperation received from personnel in our national parks, U.S. Forest Service District Ranger offices, Bureau of Land Management District Resource offices, defense department units, state parks and forests, state natural resource offices, local parks and recreation areas has been instrumental in locating the trail on the ground.

The most important element in the success of any trail, whether a local trail or a 6,000-mile trail from coast to coast is the interest and involvement of local citizens in "their trail." That pride and personal commitment from members of local trail organizations, civic groups, and local officials has been the major factor in establishing the route of the ADT.

This route was explored by a team of four people, Eric Seaborg, Ellen Dudley, Sam Carlson, and Bill Sprotte, who hiked and biked their way across the United States in 1990–91 following the route recommended by citizens in thirteen states and the District of Columbia. This scouting expedition laid the foundation upon which the ADT has developed. A second, more northerly, midwest route was established in 1993 adding Iowa and Nebraska to the ADT.

The basic route established by the scouting expedition has been refined during the past three years to take advantage of new trail projects and better trail opportunities that were either not known about or not ready for public use when the scouting team made its trip. This will be a continuing effort for many years to come as new trail opportunities are opened to the public.

Trails, like everything else, cost money. American Hiking Society members through their dues have financed a part of this project. It has been companies in the outdoor recreation industry, led by significant funding from *Backpacker* magazine, that has provided the majority of the funds to make the American Discovery Trail become a reality. An effort of the nationwide magnitude of the ADT must have coordination. That leadership has come through the fourteen state coordinators, whose guidance, trails expertise, and personal commitment has made the ADT happen.

TRAILS ORGANIZATIONS:

National:

American Hiking Society
P.O. Box 2160
Washington, DC 20041-2160

American Volkssport Association
1001 Pat Booker Road
Suite 101
Universal City, TX 78148

Rails-to-Trails Conservancy
1400 16th Street, NW
Suite 300
Washington, DC 20036

Maryland and Washington, D.C.:

Anacostia Headwaters Greenway
4112 30th Street
Mount Rainier, MD 20712-1834

Chesapeake & Ohio Canal Association
P.O. Box 366
Glen Echo, MD 20812

W B & A Recreation Trail
9430 L–S Road
Seabrook, MD 20706

Potomac Appalachian Trail Club
118 Park Street, SE
Vienna, VA 22180

West Virginia:

Appalachian Trail Conference
P.O. Box 807
Harpers Ferry, WV 25425

North Bend Rails to Trails Foundation
P.O. Box 206
Cairo, WV 26337

West Virginia Scenic Trails Association
P.O. Box 4042
Charleston, WV 25364

Ohio:

Buckeye Trail Association
P.O. Box 254
Worthington, OH 43085

North Country Trail Association
P.O. Box 311
White Cloud, MI 49349

Indiana:

Cardinal Greenway, Inc.
650 W. Minnetrista Blvd.
Muncie, IN 47303-2992

Central Indiana Wilderness Club
P.O. Box 44351
Indianapolis, IN 46244

Indianapolis Hiking Club
5176 Atherton South Drive
Indianapolis, IN 46219

Southern Indiana Hiking Club
2881 Beth Lane
Corydon, IN 47112

The Whitewater Valley Wanderers
715 College Avenue
Richmond, IN 47374

Illinois:

Friends of the I & M Canal
19 W 580 83rd
Downers Grove, IL 60516

Old Plank Road Trail
411 East Circle Drive
New Lenox, IL 60451

River to River Trail Society
1142 Winkleman Road
Harrisburg, IL 62946

Iowa:

Great River Trail
3509 Main Street
Apt. 2
Davenport, IA 52806

Heart of Iowa Trail
101 Main
Slater, IA 50244

Hoover Nature Trail
P.O. Box 123
West Liberty, IA 52776

Iowa Trails Council
P.O. Box 131
Center Point, IA 52213-0131

Linn County Trails Association
P.O. Box 2681
Cedar Rapids, IA 52406

Nebraska:

Eastern Nebraska Trails Network
P.O. Box 6725
Omaha, NE 68106

Great Plains Trails Network
5000 North 7th Street
Lincoln, NE 68521

Missouri:

Gateway Trailnet
7185 Manchester Road
St. Louis, MO 63143

Katy Trail Coalition
P.O. Box 7169
Columbia, MO 65205

Oregon-California Trail Association
P.O. Box 1019
Independence, MO 64051-0519

Kansas:

Kansas Trail Council
1737 Rural Street
Emporia, KS 66801

Santa Fe Trail Association
Santa Fe Trail Center
Route 3
Larned, KS 67550

Colorado:

Colorado Mountain Club
710 10th Street, #200
Golden, CO 80401

Colorado Trail Foundation
548 Pine Song Trail
Golden, CO 80401

Continental Divide National Scenic Trail
P.O. Box 9280
Denver, CO 80209

Pikes Peak Area Trails Coalition
P.O. Box 34
Colorado Springs, CO 80903

Volunteers for Outdoor Colorado
1410 Grant Street, Suite B
Denver, CO 80203

Utah:

Mormon Trails Association
2011 East Bryan Avenue
Salt Lake City, UT 84108-2611

Wasatch Mountain Club
888 South 200 East
Salt Lake City, UT 84106

Nevada:

National Pony Express Association, Nevada Division
P.O. Box 1643
Minden, NV 89423

California:

Bay Area Ridge Trail Council
311 California Street
Suite 300
San Francisco, CA 94104

Heritage Trails Fund
5301 Pine Hollow Road
Concord, CA 94521

Pacific Crest Trail Association
1350 Castle Rock Road
Walnut Creek, CA 94598

Tahoe Rim Trail
P.O. Box 10156
South Lake Tahoe, CA 96158

Western States Trail
380 Hayes Street
San Francisco, CA 94102

National and State Coordinators

National Coordinator:

Reese F. Lukei, Jr.
1046 Azalea Court
Virginia Beach, VA 23452

Delaware/Maryland:

Jim Ippolito
609 Savannah Rd.
Lewes, DE 19958

Maryland/District of Columbia:

Harry Cyphers
3008 Tarragon Lane
Bowie, MD 20715

West Virginia:

Lu Schrader
1202 Ridge Dr.
S. Charleston, WV 25309

Ohio/Kentucky:

Paul Daniel
7 Peabody Dr.
Oxford, OH 45056

Indiana:

Ron Craig
4303 Greenway Dr.
Indianapolis, IN 46220

Illinois (south):

John O'Dell
1142 Winkleman Rd.
Harrisburg, IL 62946

Illinois (north):

Lisa MacArtney
21 Spinning Wheel, #16C
Hinsdale, IL 60521

Missouri:

Darwin Hindman
1001 E. Walnut St., #300
Columbia, MO 65201

Iowa:

Tom Neenan
P.O. Box 131
Center Point, IA 52213

Nebraska:

Susan Rodenburg
3340 S. 29th St.
Lincoln, NE 68502

Kansas:

Dick Dilsaver
304 Stratford Rd.
Wichita, KS 67206

Colorado:

Bill Stoehr
P.O. Box 3610
3959 S. Highway 74
Evergreen, CO 80439

Utah:

Chad Johnson
48 N. Main
Beaver, UT 84713

Nevada:

Dale Ryan
649 E. Appion Way
Carson City, NV 89701

California:

John Fazel
66 Loma Vista Dr.
Orinda, CA 94563

American Hiking Society Information

American Hiking Society is a national nonprofit organization dedicated to preserving America's trails and protecting the interests of hikers. Through more than 125 affiliate clubs, AHS represents half a million trails advocates and serves as the voice of the American hiker. AHS works to educate the public in the many benefits of trails, to increase the constituency for hiking and trails, and to foster research on trail issues.

AHS is founded upon the idea of partnerships among trail volunteers, public land managers, and the business community. AHS programs and publications are designed to strengthen the network of grassroots organizations and educate trail activists on how to get involved in planning, legislation, funding, and development in their own communities. AHS is a national leader in the trail preservation effort encouraging stewardship through volunteerism in trail building and maintenance.

American Hiking Society has become the standard bearer in the effort to build a nationwide network of trails and greenways that will link the country with paths of green. This network will one day connect towns like today's highway system, but on a human, natural scale.

The plan for this network is called "Trails for All Americans." AHS is dedicated to realizing this dream shared by all American trail advocates.

Your local trail organization can support this effort by becoming an affiliate member of AHS. You can become a part of this effort and help to support the further development of the American Discovery Trail by joining AHS. Send your $25 membership check to: American Hiking Society, P.O. Box 20160, Washington, D.C. 20041-2160.

Index